As I Lay Dreaming

Poems and Micro Tales of Reveries, Memories and Dreams

Pamela Brothers Denyes

© 2022 Pamela Brothers Denyes.
All rights reserved.

This material may not be reproduced in any form, published, reprinted, recorded, performed, broadcast, rewritten or redistributed without the explicit permission of Pamela Brothers Denyes. All such actions are strictly prohibited by law.

Cover image by Johannes Plenio
Author photo by Pamela Brothers Denyes

ISBN: 978-1-7363895-0-8

Table of Contents

As I Lay Dreaming	5
Searching Remembered Rooms	6
From Where We Awaken	7
The Square Helicopter	8
Wrestling	9
Interlude	10
Before Dawn	11
A Tiny Vein Rose	12
Peace Lesson	13
Just Like Old Times	14
Becoming the Veil Nebula	15
Nana's Porch	16
Illusion, Again	17
King Vanlande's Dream or Drifa's Revenge	18
Blue Girl Dreaming	20
Listen	21
Safe in My Running	22
Dreamspace	23
À Vendre	24
His Mother Begged Me	25
Dreams of the Edge	26
Rear View Mirror	27
Concerto for a Mara	28

Angry Puckered Pout	29
Dreaming of Sister	30
Bodyless Mind	31
Random Brain Sparks	32
Rameau's Orchestra	33
Magnificent Force	34
Surprised	35
The Helper	36

As I Lay Dreaming

As I lay dreaming,
someone read a poem aloud,
about a family without anything at all.

Even their cherished home country
was not theirs anymore, lost
to greedy wars and famine.

My co-creating brain painted
a writhing blue-red ocean, raging
and roaring with human sorrows.

This gigantic emotion-wave of many
millions suffering crashed down upon
my still sleeping body,

flooding salty tears to my eyes
and the iron taste of blood
into my mouth.

Searching Remembered Rooms

Free of myself, I wandered remembered rooms,
full of people I knew or loved, or still love, amazed
to find them there, jamming together in a house I

once owned, or maybe two houses, morphed for vague
subject matter relevance, until there was just one house
with blended purposes and memories all mashed up until I

could not decipher persons or the ways I had known them.
Nor did it matter that I could not, for everyone was happy
to be playing music together. Noticing your absence, I

floated through all the rooms, the yard, to the river's edge,
searching for you, my long ago music man. Accepting
that you weren't coming, sad-but-angry tears woke me.

From Where We Awaken

"Be true to your heart,"
he writes 53 years later.

       For me, it was a sleepy summer dream,
       foolish youth and false investment.

"Time, choices, effort… Did I
try too hard, not enough?"

       Such is ever the heartbreaking
       paradox of slumberous passion.

"Least resistance leads
to temporary success…"

       What can we do with safely boxed away
       memories, the time and distance?

"There was a huge cost…
my life's course would be so different."

       So we move on
       from where we awaken.

The Square Helicopter

A huge square helicopter hovered black against the hazy summer sky, then landed in our open field down by the river's muddy edge. I ran into our Victorian fixer-upper, turned on the stained sink's faucet, which spurted reddish sludge, to wash the garden from my hands. I feared it might be some odd secret military chopper, but men in suits left the strange black helicopter, and came up to the house from the field. Whoever they were, they were dressed handsomely and would be treated well. We don't have much besides Nana's old house, but we can be hospitable.

After a few minutes of sweet tea and chit-chat, the strangers told us they wanted to use our old house for a movie location. They'd give us a lot of money to lease it, complete with the riverside section, the orchard and the gardens. It was more than enough money to repair everything. All I could think about was the sore nuisance and serious inconvenience for my neighbors. Then I remembered the nuisance plumbing and the inconvenient roof leaks. As soon as I asked them when they wanted to start, my dream ended! I woke up disoriented and oddly sad.

Now I wonder about just one thing:
Why didn't I ask them about the square helicopter?

Wrestling

It was a wrestling sleep,
all night with my own shortcomings,

more than that, the selfish ditching
by someone who's ditched me before.

My dreams grappled with forgotten things,
with anguish about a close friend.

It is certain beyond doubt, that I
have harrowing connections to loss,

body memories of being let down,
of gravely disappointing another,

struggling to rise above sad mistakes,
thoughtless actions, unwise choices,

carving the over-zealous woman I am now,
striving like the tiny wren, rebuilding

her nest each time it is raided, left broken,
empty, and she, alone again.

Interlude

Excitement builds as the orchestra begins the introduction to Rossini's Cinderella, familiar but not tired, light but not frivolous. I watch bear-strong fingers make sweet love to your dark curvy double bass, enjoying the plush seat you arranged after you said that you don't think of me as "a date."

Your bass delights at your touch, singing her deep alto notes for your pleasure and mine. I am lost in the beauty of the music and you. When you carefully lay her aside to leave the pit, I watch you, lumbering like a stiff sleepy bear to find your new friend again for the few moments of the interlude.

Because you told me where to find you, I slip from my second-row aisle seat and, like a sacred treasure hunt through labyrinthine back halls, search for you, sniffing for bear essence, that energy, your full fine frame, and I find you waiting, exactly where you chose to be found.

Your bear hug greets me, holds me longer than before. Luminous hazel eyes gaze into mine for one immeasurable moment. Long fret fingers slide down my cheek, lift my face to meet your lips in a hungry first kiss that says clearly to me, "I changed my mind."

Before Dawn

Before dawn, the world is juicy possibility,
full of honest expectation.

My mind bobs on the outgoing tide of dreams,
ready to sprout goals with wings.

Wiping dark night from yesterday's
still-starry sky, the buoyant sun crests,

responsibly opening the velvet curtain
on this one irreplaceable day.

This dancing world begins again, and I
am stronger now, if only for a little while.

A Tiny Vein Rose

I watched as a tiny vein rose into a curious little blue bubble on my left wrist, then stretched menacingly longer, pulsing blue-black blood. As the insistent vein crept toward my elbow, the part of me that was still thinking saw a blood clot forming and knew I must get to the hospital. At the ER, no one was in a hurry to help. "Stroke, it could be stroke," I cried out to anyone listening, hoping for blood thinner in time. Crazed with fear, I woke from the dream before the blue-black vein could kill me.

Peace Lesson

Some deeply internalized master teacher
lately brings me clever lessons disguised
in nearly every simple thing I do.

Today as I walked in a public garden, full
of honest wonder at the turning season, I felt
annoyed by constantly chattering youngsters.

I turned instead to the Japanese Garden, the most
reverently quiet space for me. Soon the gong there
reverberated under a child's eager hand and I heard,

> "You must carry your own peace with you,
> everywhere you go. Wear it like an unseen
> garment that girds and protects you."

Just Like Old Times

You ordered my favorite Italian dishes at Anna's, without having to ask me, and a very good red wine. So long ago, but you remembered! When the garlic knots came, you gave me the first choice of their buttery deliciousness. Your usual order was long coming from the busy kitchen, but you would not allow them to hold my meal, so I savored my manicotti marinara as you chatted and guzzled several cold beers.

Everything was just like old times
until I woke from the dream,
feeling so hungry for you.

Becoming the Veil Nebula

Not remembering how it all happened
feels like a blessing now,

but I still have very strange crashing
dreams about a violent surging

E.X..P...L….O…..S…...I…….O……..N,

metamorphosing to a sparkling vaporous
thread flowing into the broad universe,

neither wave nor particle, only the glow
that was once alive as something else.

Nana's Porch

Turning into Nana's driveway I was surprised to see so many cars. Her crumbling Victorian garage held no car since PaPa died in '58. I often drove the fifty miles to see her, to be with her comforting smile. This time there was silence as I entered Nana's back door through the kitchen.

Auntie Jo floated down the perfect staircase, passing just in front of the tabletop display of family photos, in neat rows, back to front, large to small. I asked her about the extra cars and she said, "We're all here for our Nana's funeral. Oh, my dear… you didn't know? No one told you?"

Receding like a ghost, I floated backward through the living room, onto the side porch, angry-crying for some time, on Nana's ancient glider. Silently the glass-paned door opened and out came Nana, only her hair was dark chestnut again, and her clothing bright red and navy.

She softly said that she is just fine, not to be sad, nor to fret at all, because the line between life and death is thin as a fine tulle veil. Nothing about her love for me had changed, Nana said, and told me to focus on the love I had for her and she would always be there beside me—still loving me.

When Nana actually passed from this life six months later, I found great comfort in the memory of that sweet dream visitation, already stored in my heart.

Illusion, Again

The I whom I know came back
into my body very suddenly.

Startled, I gasped for air, as though I had
held my breath for a month, or pulled up
out of a deep sea dive, needing real air.

For a moment the world was grey
and low light, no colors in sight.

Another deep breath brought back the colors
of simple treasures in the room I know as mine,
where last night I thrived in illusion, again.

You were there.
Did you have the same dream?

King Vanlande's Dream
or Drifa's Revenge

King Vanlande of Upsal took me as his lawful wife,
given by my good father, Snae the Old, as is our
custom. Taking my bed for the winter, I was his
alone and glad for our fruitful joining.

When springtime came to Finland, my own king
and husband took his leave, promising to be absent
from me, his grieving queen and the child I would
soon bear him, for no more than three years.

Three years turned into six and then ten, with no
husband or king in my bed. Had I been forgotten
by a foolish man or was he still thinking I should
wait upon a king who considers me chattel?

Maddened by the angry grief of empty years–nine
lost years for his son, seven years of his promise
broken–I sent his son, whom I alone named Visbur,
away to the royal courts of his father's Sweden.

Then I called to me the witch-wife Huld, and bribed
her that she should find my missing husband
and bewitch him to come home to me, or else
finish his life for him.

Finding him at home in Upsal, she bewitched him
for a little while, making him wish to come back
to Finland. Vanlande's kinsmen and scheming
counsellors advised him not to come to me.

Therefore Huld made the king unusually and deeply
sleepy, and take to his bed to find rest. But there
he found no rest at all, for soon Huld became
the invisible dream-witch Mara.

She trampled his body until he cried out. His aides
strove to fight the Mara, which they could neither
see nor feel, as she broke their king's chest, his legs,
then danced upon his head.

Thus negligent King Vanlande died a vicious death,
trampled by the feet of the Mara, the witch-wife's
own wicked tool.

When she returned to tell it, I rewarded her richly,
then poured my mad self into the frigid waters
of the Gulf of Bothnia to slay my sorrow.

Blue Girl Dreaming

Am I a girl
dreaming that
I am a blue flower?

Or am I a blue flower
dreaming that
I am a girl?

These things are
difficult to know
for certain,

And I feel so doubtful
that I am entirely
one or the other.

Listen

Because all my life's answers
call to me from the woods,
I walk here and listen…to everything.

I watch for shifts and shapes, for light
to change, for some honest meaning
to make life clearer, breathing easier.

Today fog descends, shrouding the trees,
my view, cooling the fragrant blossoms.
Even the birds sing out to welcome it.

No wind will move this cloud mass
until day break, so I walk on in the damp
over-layer closing in swiftly, listening.

Moist fog has its virtues, after all.
I breathe in the mist deeply, releasing
my desire to escape its gentle wrap.

Birds call to each other until the very last
moment of the fog's incoming creep,
chirping and feeding in soft grayness.

Finally the fog, thick as cream soup,
overwhelms the woods. Even the birds
are silent again, and all is still.

What answer did I hear?
I don't remember the question!

Safe in My Running

I allowed our conversation to crawl up into my head,
so there you danced around in my dreams all night.

> Something you said or did scared me, challenged me
> so hard that I ran away from you. I took only my phone
> and car, and promptly got lost in higher-than-true hills
> around Richmond.
>
> I couldn't leave town until I picked up my suitcase, but
> in my fear and anger, I could not remember the
> location of the hotel and panicked. I found myself
> crying on a cliff, looking down at oddly wide white
> buildings.
>
> Just as I remembered that the reservation was still on
> my phone, you came up behind me, trying to assure me
> that everything would be okay, but I was still wary.
> How did you find me…?

As often happens in dreams, as soon as I
asked the question I knew the answer.

> You came after me.
> I had run away the very first time something got sticky
> between us, and you followed me, making sure I was
> safe in my running, to lead me out of my fear.
>
> No one has done that before.
> Ever.

A lump in my throat and cold tears on my cheek woke me,
with the certainty that something big has shifted.

Dreamspace

It only happens when I cannot feel my body around my being: sometimes sleeping, sometimes meditating. Then I am comfortable and empty of concern about anything at all. I know that I am I, can recognize people in the dream, and can make decisions for the part of me that is in the dreamspace. It has become clear to me that in these moments, I may meet someone who has passed from this life. My open awareness leaves a space for them to slip into a dream my mind creates around them.

Today I met a little boy in one of these dreams. He came to my home twice. The second time, I found him tucked up into a bookshelf, napping, as little children can do anywhere. When I came in, he woke and wished to be near me, saying I was the only one who understood. Somehow I knew his body was not alive, but here he was!

The lad showed me the direction of the house where he had lived. He was my neighbor's child, whom I did not know had died. Hoping I could talk to his mother for him, he came to visit me in my dream. Over and over, the little boy told me how concerned he was about her. I comforted him as we plotted how to get his mother down to my house so we could talk to her.

As happens in reveries, it all melted away when I awoke from the dreamspace. I must get to know the family better. The last time I had one of these dreams, it was my grandmother who had come to tell me that death isn't at all what we think, and that, though she is dead, she will always be as near as a thought to me. Nana came into my dreamspace six months before she passed away, to give me the peace I would need when it happened. I must call the little boy's mother today.

À Vendre

"For sale," the sign calls to me in French,
summer's lacy curtains barely veiling
ancient windows, neatly framed by honest
well-tended red geraniums.

At the crown of the house, the rooftop patio,
I'll sip my wine and watch this river's
temporary residents wondering who I am,
what riverside stories live here with me.

They won't know that I, too, wonder
who I am. What did I come here to find?
Perhaps to immerse or maybe to isolate,
to examine life through a lighter veil?

Ah, will I really move this far away, only
to observe myself in the unvarnished mirror
of French culture? To become another colorful
story in this apartment's history?

His Mother Begged Me

His mother (but not his mother) begged me to leave him alone, asking "Are you here to hurt him again, to make him cry again?" With fierce urgency in my voice, I told her that I had to see him, to tell him something I should have said years ago: I am ready to be his wife! I promised her that I would love and care for him always. Because that's what she'd wanted for us, she allowed me to come into her home (but not his mother's home).

To get to the room where my lover was, I faced a test: I had to climb a strangely slack canvas ladder. Inexplicably, a younger friend, just finished with his Basic Training, came to my aid. Using a strong double-forearm grip, he finally got me to the top, just as a gunshot rang out.

    "No, not when I'm so close!" I screamed.

Stunned by the horrible thought that my lover had shot himself, I woke up, and realized that the shooter was just outside my own window.

Dreams of the Edge

Spring, with her moody beauty,
with her quicksilver stormy weather,
dreamed of hot dry days, puffy clouds,
dancing nights as light as a feather.

Summer, arid without a drop, first
could not sleep for incessant heat,
then in exhaustion, dreamed of autumn,
himself prostrate at her chilly feet.

Autumn flowed with gentler winds
and rain enough for harvest's best,
but in her secret dreams one night
was shown she needed winter's rest.

Winter rose with a roaring chill,
blasting away warm harvest days.
One long harsh night he secretly dreamed
of warming green, of sweet spring's ways.

And so we dreamers will view this life,
each edge a welcoming season's change,
through storms, arid heat, bounty and rest.
That, no elegant wisdom can rearrange.

Rear View Mirror

In the dream I hurried along to somewhere. I was driving on the down side of a hill, starting to pull up another, on a narrow two-lane road. As a semi whizzed past, I checked my rear view mirror. A terrified gut-punch hit me, as I saw a kid in a box-car racer pull out at the hilltop behind me, heading straight into the semi, with little control, only a hand brake. After a heart-breaking gasp, I put my eyes back on my own path, averting my attention from a certain horrible scene that I could do nothing about, except to make a conscious decision to keep going, to not look back at the horror that was not mine to handle today.

Concerto for a Mara

The Shostakovich last night quaked, blistering
background music for a Mara. Concerto no. 1
in C minor for piano, trumpet and strings, opus 35,

so perfectly written that the piano's scherzo notes
and schizo rhythms pranced the stage fiendishly,
the orchestra a rolling black ocean beneath it.

A horn soloist tooted unexpected pronouncements
or held very long notes at the oddest moments,
disjointed but so very moving, as odd dreams can be.

It sat on my chest purring and broke my heart.

Angry Puckered Pout

In the dream, I spent all day next door at the young neighbor's, with the new baby. I wandered over to check on her and stayed during a sudden crazy-for-spring snowstorm, complete with thunder and lightning, hail hitting our cars, a power outage, feet of snow, trouble with baby latching on, her older child jealously acting out, a nagging sense I had to be somewhere, and me barefoot.

    Nonsense.

I scampered home barefooted and there you were, conducting a meeting at the kitchen table with your whole face wrinkled into an angry puckered pout. Ladies wandering the house told me how happy they were that we were finally getting married, which you had not told me yet. I thought, wow, one day away in all these years, he's horribly upset and *now* he's ready to marry?

    Crazy, huh?

Today it's been nine years since you died. When I awoke, I realized that I had forgotten your angry puckered pout, how you seemed able to combine all of your feelings on your face at one time–you are so precious, you hurt me terribly, I love you, how can I forgive you–all over your eyes and mouth. That's when I understood that you hadn't shown me that face in the last few years of our marriage…

    and I cried again.

Dreaming of Sister

Tied up like twins
in a small womb,

we writhed and
we stretched,

and together
we pushed hard

against the walls
holding us away

from our mother,
never expecting

to live worlds
apart from her,

you, physically and
I, emotionally.

Bodyless Mind

My bodyless mind dreamed,
and I was flying, rolling,

cruising clouds, dipping,
diving, far and away, no matter

that my arms and legs seemed
of no use in these acrobatics,

were maybe not even there.

I sensed a memory, some broadly
psycho-physical remembrance,

that I have or had limbs,
but my new bodyless mind

no longer needed
what I had grudgingly

carried with me everywhere,
up until then.

Random Brain Sparks

He gazed hungrily at me for a long time,
saying that he simply could not turn away.
Even though it was only a dream,
I smiled differently for a week.

I dreamed a daring rescue,
with good help from other brave souls.
Now I believe that I am stronger
in heart and mind to handle new risks.

Dreaming: is it random brain sparks
or memory formation, shifting storage bins,
preserving brain plasticity, or perhaps
insight into hidden depths of psyche?

Every dream appears so very real because
we seem to feel the feelings in each one
and seem to see it all with our own…

With our own what?

Rameau's Orchestra

Astonished, I find myself suddenly in fancy dress,
hearing a small orchestra tuning for Rameau.
Scanning the dim hall, I wonder why I am here.

Flute, violin, then throaty cello and French horn
sing together, sparkling the air around each player
with every tooting triplet and draw of bow.

Translucent colors paint the stage, lighting the hall
as everyone wonders at the bright spectacle. Patrons
in their boxes smile, pleased with the strange concert.

Rameau's enchanted music brightens the old hall, now
glowing carpet to rafters. Baffled players, instruments
and curious audience begin to hover and dance!

Buoyant and dancing delightedly, I laugh, performing
a mid-air jig with the handsome bear of a bass player,
finally awakening with a smile, humming Rameau.

Magnificent Force

Six hundred years old! She dreamed that she would live
to be six hundred years old, and believes it.

So when the tumor had to be removed from her brain stem,
she knew it was not her end, no matter what doctors said.

How could a one-time brain storage activity, a dream
from thirty-five years ago, make a person lose   all   fear,

hold so tightly to her own dream-generated expectations?
What magnificent force is this?

Surprised

Startled to see you, I woke up gasping,
quilted in the warmth of sound sleep,
instantly wanting to call you.

I still need to ask if you're okay,
to know if you need me there.

When you show up in a dream,
or some sudden urgent memory,
it's like licking an envelope:

I'm always surprised by the taste
but not that the glue is there.

The Helper

From a distance I saw a glow around him.
He looked maybe seventy or so, with almost
translucent white hair, and like someone
I should know, but not entirely.

All of his loose-fitting clothing was white, too.
As he came nearer, I did not see wrinkles
in his skin, nor any flaw. I said hello
and asked his name.

"I used to have a name," he said, "but
it's gone now, and I don't really miss it."

       Wait… did he actually *say* that
       or did I just hear it?

The glow around him brightened
as I realized we were not speaking,
but communicating with each other
by pure intention.

I felt comfortable and warm,
as my own body began to glow.

Asking what he does, I heard only,
"I am a helper now, here to help you.
Relax and allow your life to be smoother.
Relax and allow… Relax and allow…"

I awoke feeling so very calm,
with just a little more glow than usual.

       Was it you?

Grateful acknowledgement is given to the following books, literary journals and anthologies where some of the poems in this book were first published:

Calling the Beginning: "King Vanlande's Dream, or Drifa's Revenge"

Fauxmoir Literary Magazine: "Searching Remembered Rooms"

Field of Black Roses: "As I Lay Dreaming"

I Have a Dream: "Safe in My Running"

Journal of Blue Ridge Writers: "Interlude," "From Where We Awaken"

The Right Mistakes: "À Vendre," "Concerto for a Mara," "Listen," "Peace Lesson"

The Widow's Lovers: "Angry Puckered Pout," "Surprised"

Vanish in Poetry: "The Helper"

Virginia Writers Club Golden Nib Journal: "Dreams of the Edge"

About the Author

Pamela's award-winning poems are published in several Virginia writers' journals, Wingless Dreamer, Barstow & Grand V, several international collections by The Poet Magazine, Vallum Poetry and more. Her first two poetry books, *The Right Mistakes* and *The Widow's Lovers,* will be published in 2022 by Kelsay Books.

Pamela's career-based writing included contract nonfiction, instructional design and manuals, developmental and copy editing, and online/print writing for her regional newspaper and internet gateway. She is also a musician and singer, and has worked professionally in that arena, too. A mother and grandmother, Pamela resides in eastern Virginia but travels all she can.

Artist's Statement

Retired now, I am harvesting forty years of poetry, song-writing, journals and travelogues to create new works—and fun! I am inspired by creative arts of every stripe, and most especially the natural world. The brevity of form in poetry is the most immediately accessible type of art when that inspiration comes to me. A daily writer for a very long time, my affirmation is "May I never cease to be amazed!"

Made in the USA
Middletown, DE
01 September 2023